AWESOME ANIMAL HEROES

EUGENIE CLARK

REBECCA FELIX

Consulting Editor, Diane Craig, M.A./Reading Specialist

Super Sandcastle

An Imprint of Abdo Publishing
abdopublishing.com

abdopublishing.com

Published by Abdo Publishing, a division of ABDO, PO Box 398166, Minneapolis, Minnesota 55439. Copyright © 2017 by Abdo Consulting Group, Inc. International copyrights reserved in all countries. No part of this book may be reproduced in any form without written permission from the publisher. Super SandCastle™ is a trademark and logo of Abdo Publishing.

Printed in the United States of America, North Mankato, Minnesota
102016
012017

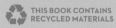
Editor: Paige Polinsky
Content Developer: Nancy Tuminelly
Cover and Interior Design and Production: Mighty Media, Inc.
Photo Credits: 0076107-DSH © David Shen/SeaPics.com, AP Images, John Consoli/University of Maryland, John F. Williams/Office of Naval Research, National Geographic, Shutterstock, Tak Konstantinou, WalterPro4755/Flickr

Publisher's Cataloging-in-Publication Data

Names: Felix, Rebecca, author.
Title: Eugenie Clark / by Rebecca Felix.
Description: Minneapolis, MN : Abdo Publishing, 2017. | Series: Awesome animal heroes
Identifiers: LCCN 2016944698 | ISBN 9781680784329 (lib. bdg.) | ISBN 9781680797855 (ebook)
Subjects: LCSH: Clark, Eugenie--Juvenile literature. | Ichthyologists--United States--Biography--Juvenile literature. | Marine biologists--United States--Biography--Juvenile literature.
Classification: DDC 597/.092 [B]--dc23
LC record available at http://lccn.loc.gov/2016944698

Super SandCastle™ books are created by a team of professional educators, reading specialists, and content developers around five essential components—phonemic awareness, phonics, vocabulary, text comprehension, and fluency—to assist young readers as they develop reading skills and strategies and increase their general knowledge. All books are written, reviewed, and leveled for guided reading, early reading intervention, and Accelerated Reader™ programs for use in shared, guided, and independent reading and writing activities to support a balanced approach to literacy instruction.

CONTENTS

THE SHARK LADY

Eugenie Clark was an ichthyologist. This type of scientist studies fish. Clark is best known for her work with sharks. She swam with sharks. She studied them. Clark became known as the Shark Lady. She taught people about these misunderstood creatures.

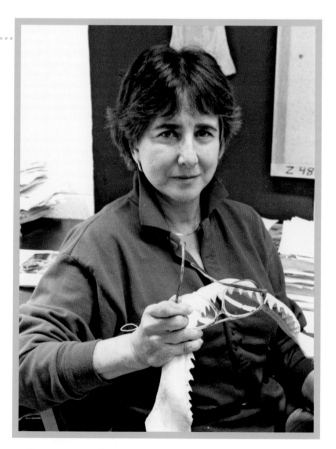

Eugenie Clark

EUGENIE CLARK

BORN: May 4, 1922, New York City

MARRIED: Jideo Umaki (1942–1947), Ilias Konstantinou (1950–1967), Chandler Brossard (1967–1969), Igor Klatzo (1970), Henry Yoshinobu Kon (1997–2000)

CHILDREN: Hera Konstantinou, Aya Konstantinou, Themistokles "Tak" Konstantinou, Nikolas Konstantinou

DIED: February 25, 2015

EARLY LIFE

Eugenie Clark was born in 1922 in New York City. Her father died when she was a baby. Eugenie's mother, Yumiko, raised her. Yumiko was Japanese. The sea is important in Japanese **culture**. Young Eugenie loved the ocean.

Eugenie's grandmother often told her Japanese ghost stories.

Eugenie grew up on Long Island, an island in New York City. It is currently the most populated island in the United States.

AQUARIUM ADVENTURES

At age nine, Eugenie visited the New York Aquarium. There, she saw large tanks of fish. She was delighted. Eugenie returned to the aquarium often. She watched the sharks. She imagined she was swimming with them.

Young Eugenie loved to visit the New York Aquarium. Today, visitors can observe more than 8,000 different animals there.

SEA STUDIES

Clark graduated from high school in 1938. She studied **zoology** in college. In 1942, she graduated and married Jideo Umaki. After four more years of school, Clark was ready to explore the sea. She took diving **research** trips around the world.

Clark received her master's degree from New York University.

Clark traveled to the Red Sea for her first major **research** project. This body of water lies between Africa and Asia.

BREAKING BARRIERS

In 1946, Clark began working at Scripps **Institution** of **Oceanography**. She was one of only two women there. At the time, female oceanographers were limited. They were not allowed to go on dangerous dives. Clark worked hard to prove herself.

Clark was especially interested in triggerfish.

The Scripps **Institution** is in California. Today, it uses the FLoating Instrument Platform (FLIP) to study the ocean.

FISH AND FAMILY

Clark and Umaki divorced in 1947. Clark continued traveling, studying ocean fish. She became a brave diver. In 1950, Clark earned a doctorate degree. She also married Ilias Konstantinou. They had two sons and two daughters. Clark brought her children along on **research** trips.

Clark discovered the Red Sea Moses sole, a type of small fish.

TRAINING SHARKS

A wealthy family heard about Clark's work. The Vanderbilts started a **research** lab in Florida. They made Clark its director. Clark made many discoveries there. In 1956, she trained lemon sharks in the lab's pools! Until then, people thought sharks were unintelligent. Clark's work changed that.

Clark's lab was named the Mote Marine Laboratory and Aquarium.

TEACHER AND EXPLORER

In 1968, Clark began teaching. She taught **marine biology** at the University of Maryland. Meanwhile, Clark discovered many new types of fish. In 1973, she studied "sleeping sharks" in Mexico. Scientists thought sharks had to keep moving in order to breathe. But Clark proved this wrong.

The sleeping sharks were Caribbean reef sharks.

In Mexico, Clark dove into caves full of sleeping sharks.

SEA HERO

Clark took her last dive in 2014.

Clark taught the public about sharks. She also spoke about protecting the ocean. In 2004, Clark learned she had lung **cancer**. But she continued working. Clark died in 2015. Over her lifetime, she led more than 200 **research** trips. She changed the way people saw ocean wildlife.

MORE ABOUT CLARK

In 1981, Clark dove with WHALE SHARKS. They are the largest ocean fish. Clark rode on the back of one of these giants!

Clark learned how to swim before she was TWO YEARS OLD.

Clark often talked to fishermen while traveling. They taught her about the area's SEA CREATURES.

TEST YOUR KNOWLEDGE

1. Where did Clark often watch sharks swimming as a child?

2. Clark trained lemon sharks. True or false?

3. How many **research** trips did Clark lead during her life?

THINK ABOUT IT!

What is your favorite ocean animal? Why?

ANSWERS: 1. The New York Aquarium   **2.** True   **3.** More than 200

GLOSSARY

cancer – a disease that causes some cells in the body to grow faster than normal and attack healthy organs and tissues.

culture – the ideas, traditions, art, and behaviors of a group of people.

institution – a large organization where people live or work together.

marine biology – the study of the plants and animals that live in the ocean.

oceanography – the study of oceans, seas, and marine life. A person who studies oceanography is an oceanographer.

research – a study of something to learn new information.

zoology – a branch of biology that deals with animals and their behavior.